The Umbilical Cord:
Poems and Prose
By
A Mother and Son
Geneva Blair and Edward Blair

M.O.R.E. Publishers
St. Louis, MO

1

The Umbilical Cord:

Poems and Prose
By
A Mother and Son
Geneva Blair and Edward Blair

Printed in the United States
ISBN 978-1-945344-03-9
Library of Congress Control Number: 2016940524

Edited by Edwin M.T. Grider and Angelee Grider
M.O.R.E. Publishers CO, Memphis (TN)

INTRODUCTION
(...MOTHER AND SON)
By Edward Blair

This little book of prose and poetry is a compilation of original works by a mother and her son.

In attempting to discover a title that would best describe the spirit of this book, I began to think about my relationship with my mother. I realized that had it not been for her struggles to bring me forth in birth, and then provide me with the sustaining nurture that would help shape my entire life, my sense of being and sense of self would never have been developed. Nor my love for poetry, such as she herself had, would have ever been realized.

The book is therefore an outgrowth of what my mother and I shared: she carrying the child; the child receiving all from being carried. When she ate, I ate. What she drank, I drank. When she thought, I had to be part of the process of development - broken off and absorbed.

It is true! I believe that something passes between the two, mother and child, to which fathers cannot relate. They beam over the result. She beams over the process. This, I believe, helps shape the child; molds, and to a degree, determines what the child may become. I'm glad it's like that!

As I, my mother had a story to tell. Many of the readers might be able to identify with the experiences. Overall, my mother was a gifted woman. She was gifted as a mother, writer, cook and as a mother and wife.

Her story of historical events began in the late fifties when my mother was approached by one of the State of Missouri Welfare caseworkers. Unfortunately, this particular caseworker looked at her as a <u>case number</u>, not as a person, to qualify for 'welfare'.

Mother was informed by this social worker that she "must do several things." The most onerous was that she could have no man in her house! Of course that meant for all her children, they would be without a father! So, for the sake of her children during the times we lived in and to provide the necessity to survive, she consented.

My father was told the news by her. What was he to do? In spite of his objection he obeyed the misguided law. He did as he was told. He left his family.

We never saw him except when he on occasions, would sneak back into St. Louis from Chicago. He would only stay a day and leave again.

We grew up without his presence, his input, direction, guidance and fatherly figure.

The boys, were deprived most of all. There were no ball games, no discipline, no knot tying, no girl talk, and none of the chastisement all boys need.

Amazingly though my mother never divorced him. They remained married for all those years until, he died. I was told that he had become saved many years later – something my mother desperately wanted.

As a young child, I didn't understand the implications of the law – separation of family for food. I just wanted my father in our home.

Fortunately, the anger has passed. My love for him...well it will always remain because, he did what the law said he had to do. I thank him for that. Ironically, he saved his family by his absence. Also during those times of being apart, my mother wrote.

Her poems are the expressions of what she saw, what she experienced in life, and what she became in life. The poems were her foundations - upon her foundation of God and what He meant to her throughout her lifetime.

The poetry she wrote, she wanted to share with any reader the greatness of her salvation and her experiences. Those writings are entered here as she, the author, wrote and as she wanted to share with the readers. I believe she succeeded.

I, as her son, love poetry because of what it says to me. The almost mystical reasoning found in rhyme and prose is, for me the writer, the residue of the umbilical cord.

So please enjoy. We both hope (she up there, me here with you) that in these pages, you may find laughter, peace, introspection, a piece of yourself. Also our hope is that you will come to know an appreciation for the Creator, and a love of poetry and prose.

TABLE OF CONTENTS

Introduction
Her Biographical Note   11
His Biographical Note   13
Rationale   14

THE JOURNEY STARTS:
Writings of Geneva Blair
While Waiting On The Train   17
Thanksgiving   19
A Teenager's Prayer   20
The Sinner and the Hypocrite   22
Old Woman Thinks   25
Blood Serum   27
Life Insurance   29
My Christmas Gift   31
A Sinner's Plea   33
Company   35
Thank God For The Devil   37
An Old Man's Memories   39
Bible School Is Over   41
No Weapon   43
They Just Went On Ahead   46
Applying For A Home   48
Going Home   50
Peculiar People   52
The Verdict is Yours   54

To the Man of God   56
Name Brand   58
Help Wanted – Women Only   60
The Big Party   63
The Victim Rap Song   65

THE JOURNEY CONTINUES:
Writings of Edward Blair

Job	67
Judas	69
Lazarus	71
Mary	73
The Crown	75
Still, I Miss You	77
Caress	79
My Cushion	80
Hers	81
My Daughter's Hand	83
Calvary	85
My Mother's Bed	87
Ruth	89
Moods	91
Samson!	93
Resurrection Victory	96
From A Soldier's Perspective	99
Moses	101
The Victor	104
The Word	106
The Twelve	107
The Son of God	109
The King Who Stayed Home	111
When Hearts Knit	113
Body Count	115
My Grandmother's Quilt	117
My Idol	121
Old Glory	124
Remember	126

My Name is DEATH   129
My Attempt at Rhyme and Prose   131
My Name is LOVE   132
The Market Block   134
Elegy on a Monument   136
The Cruise Ship   138
An Egg With No Sperm   141
My Name is FEAR   143
His Passing   146
How She Slew Me   149
My Brother   151
My Name is PRAYER   154
Viet Nam, Give Me Back My Friend   156
Little Black Boy   158
My Name is GUN   161
Reason for Pain   165
Her Passing   166

Geneva Blair (mother)   **Edward Blair (son)**

http://www.Naturallypr.wix.com/genevascroll

https://www.createspace.com/6263788

HER BIOGRAPHICAL NOTE

My mother was born May 3, 1916 in Fordyce, Arkansas. She was the proud mother of twelve children. Her life was a mixture of the hope, dreams, and aspirations which most people experience as they go through life, except she had twelve children to share those things with.

After rearing her children alone without the attendance of a husband or father figure for the children being there with her, she enrolled in a cooking course which she completed after several months of attendance.

She then became a volunteer for the Missouri Baptist Hospital in St. Louis, Missouri. After a number of years of continuous service in the capacity of volunteer, she was hired at the hospital as a Physical Therapist's Therapy Aide. After the hospital, which was located in the City of St. Louis, moved its operations 20 miles away, into the County of St. Louis, my mother commuted via a city transit bus. She would leave home at 5:00 A.M. in order to be at work at 8:00 A.M. She established an unblemished record of job performance and attendance. She retired in June 1983 at the age of 68 and was acclaimed by her former co-workers as an "outstanding" employee.

She was also an avid writer. On several successive Christmas Holidays, she would write, produce, and direct three act plays at her church. She would also sew the clothing for each actor's costume, supply the props and.... feed the cast after the play! Each year, her plays were anticipated with an air of joy. She died in the summer of 1986, asleep in her bed.

In this book, several of my poems are recollections of the 'grand old lady', that I alone, of all her children, was allowed to call by her nickname of "Brit." In her picture on the cover, she is wearing that beautiful hat she made. This is she. I hope you will like her work.

I love you, Brit

HIS BIOGRAPHICAL NOTE

My name is Edward Blair, commonly referred to as Ed. Poetry has been a kind of therapy for me for many, many years. The first poem that gave me an impetus to even start writing was Thomas Gray's "Elegy in a County Graveyard." I love the rhythm of the cadence, the meaning behind the prose that must be searched out, and the interpretations that are to be drawn from them by the readers.

I grew up in St. Louis, Missouri, a city that cultivated in me a love for candor and quick wit. Having grown up for the most part in a housing project called Pruitt-Igoe (or as we called the 'jects'), I became captivated by the hectic city life. This was a life that was fast and unrelenting, where everything was bargained for, sometimes even life itself.

My poetry reflects, through a prism, these experiences of and through my life. As I witness something, I write about it. I try to give it purpose, but never a meaning that the reader must do.

Rationale

The Umbilical Cord: Poems and Prose by a Mother and Son is a small book that attempts to show what the writers felt and sensed about life as they observed it in all its many facets.

My previous book, entitled **Over the Backyard Fence**, is a more extensive work on my life as seen from a very unique perspective.

We (I speak for her) both hope that you will enjoy the purpose and the efforts of the work involved, and that it gives to God His just acclaim.

Enjoy.

The Journey Starts

Writings of Geneva Blair

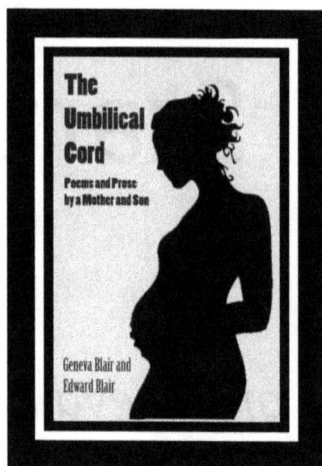

The
Umbilical
Cord

Poems and Prose
by a Mother and Son

Geneva Blair and
Edward Blair

WHILE WAITING ON THE TRAIN

I'm only on a visit here.
I haven't long to stay.

When I get word to come on home
then I must be on my way.

I won't just throw my time away -
I'll see what I can do
to try and get someone else
to travel with me too.

I'll go and visit with the sick;
leave them a word of cheer;
then help those other lonely ones
that also stopped by here.

I'll go and worship at this Church -
It's not a handsome place.
But I like the spirit that dwells in there
and its name of "Saved by Grace."

A social club wants me to join;
I'll say no to its invitation.
They don't believe in the Holy Ghost
and they ridicule my salvation!

Some laughed when I started this journey.
They called me crazy too.
But if nobody travels with me,
still, I'm going through!

THANKSGIVING

Oh, give thanks to the Lord,
for His great plan of grace;
for sending His son
to redeem this poor race.

Oh, thank Him for His loving way.
He has protected yours and mine;
shielding from dangers, seen and unseen
by His wonderful shield of love!

Oh, give thanks to the Lord
for His saints everywhere;
for the fellowship sweet,
and His love and His care.

Oh, thank Him for the food we eat
And for food that feeds our souls.
Thank Him for that 'water' inside
springing up, keeping us whole!

Taking us out of darkness
into His marvelous light:
Thank God for making us witnesses
in the power of His great might!

A TEENAGER'S PRAYER

Dear Lord, my thoughts are so confused.
My mind in much unrest.

I want to serve you as I should.
I want to do my best.

It seems the world, with all its charms,
makes everything just glow, and when I think
"Should I give in?" something tells me "no!"

I think, "I'll go to my elders to ask them for
advice". But when I see their examples I say,
"Is this the way of Christ?"

Oh, Lord, I just can't understand what I'm
supposed to do. It seems I'm such a failure,
trying to follow you.

Is religion just for 'grown ups'? Who takes
time with us? Please, teach me how to live;
teach me who to trust.

The world has many traps to keep us in its
clutch. But the Church only says "don't do".
After that is when it hushes.

Dear Lord, I'm not too dumb to know that we have souls to save. But we like to feel they love us too, to make us care and behave. They think their obligation stops when we are clothed and fed; then how can we ever learn of You, unless we're daily fed?

So, Lord, I've heard you answer prayers.
I've heard you are children's friend.
Today I'm asking for your help.

This is a teenager's prayer...
Amen!

THE SINNER AND THE HYPOCRITE

The sinner and the hypocrite had a talk one day.
As they started for a walk,
said the sinner, "I can get more folks than you with all your fancy talk."

"No," said the hypocrite, "you don't know the many, many ways that I can show.
I can win many over with nothing in sight and they'll think they're doing everything right."

"Now wait," smiled the sinner. "You just listen: I can make things sparkle until they glisten. They all like a good time and music that swings, and the girls will pay dearly for pretty things.
I can get a lot of folks into the shows by telling them it's great and everybody goes.
And if I want some immodest romancing,
I'll just start some music and that starts them dancing."

"Well," said the hypocrite, "that may be.
I don't have to do a thing, but let them watch me!
You only get the sinner to follow you;
But I can get sinners and the Church folk too.
I make them think I'm a God sent man.
I then have them eating out of my hand.
I just display a great disposition and nobody questions my position.

If they're sisters I want to entice, I'll just pat 'em and they say 'he's nice.'
I go in their home like a good friend, and brother, that's when the fun begins!"

The sinner said, "Man, you got a good scheme: That's the best set-up I ever seen!
But I can get folks and don't have to search.
But man, I sure wouldn't fool with the church!
There are drunks and gamblers I put on my side and so many liars, I couldn't divide.
All I do is make sin look pretty;
I get so many folks, boy, it's a pity!"

"Well," said the hypocrite, with a big old smirk, "I like being the 'big wheel' in that

church. I like them to think I'm a holy saint,
when all the time, I know I ain't!
If they believe I'm good, that ain't my grief.
I interpret the Bible for my belief!
It say, 'don't let the right hand know what
the left will do';
As long as I do that, who can say I'm not
true?"

"You know," said the sinner, "there's a lot I
do; but, to all of it, I have been true.
Folks like you must make God sick.
I'd rather be a sinner than a hypocrite!"

OLD WOMAN THINKS

I'm taken off my feet at this new generation.
They are the strangest folks in God's big creation.
It's not the folks in the world so much -
it's the ones who claim they belong to the church!

The Preacher's not saying anything revealing
- guess he's scared he'll hurt someone's feelings.

The choir has a sour look on their face - guess
they never heard of Amazing Grace.

The Deacons are sitting with a roving eye;
lusting after women who just prance bye.

And the sisters, they ain't helping none
because the way they dress says, "I won't run."
And some of them sisters are old as me;
trying to look a' age they will never be.
You just ask them, "Wasn't the old religion fine?"
They just say, "Sorry, before my time!"

Talking about children running wild -
it's the Ma and Pa's fault, and not the child's!
For the 23rd Psalms, they don't know where
to look,
but they can tell you everything in a comic
book.
The only way they will learn the Golden Rule
- some dear teacher taught them in school.
Just ask one of them, "Come, let's pray."
They will stop giving you the 'time of day.'

Talk about men being the head -
somebody's got to lead them instead!
Because when they are full of that stuff that
foams,
someone better show them how to get
home!

You know, it kind of puzzles me how these
folks say they are from sin set free.
Now it's not for me to judge or refute
but they sure are bearing some peculiar
fruit!
When I think of how God sent His Son to die,
I just want to hang my head and cry.
And when I see how folks continue to sin,
I wonder would He do it again?

BLOOD SERUM

It seems to be the style today -
to depend on drugs to keep disease away.

Nearly everyone's taking shots;
some in small doses, some a lot!

There are shots when you are big and fat
to keep your weight right where it's at.
There are shots to keep you nice and thin.
Drugs they use to catch the men.

There are shots to take when you can't sleep
and shots to take to make you eat;
shots to build your appetite;
also drugs to help your failing sight!

Then when you want to lose all hope,
they will sell you shots full of dope!
 shots to make your pressure decrease and
shots so your family won't increase.

Of all the shots and drugs they call,
they don't guarantee a cure at all!
But I know a serum that's tried and true,
and will cure anything that's wrong with you.

The serum is called the Blood of Christ!
For He paid a Fabulous Price!

For those other drugs, bought and never get
thru.
But he's offering this serum, free to you.

It will never stop flowing, by any means,
And will help keep your desires clean.

The serum will also correct your sight.
It will make you see things in a righteous
light.

The disease of sin, it will completely cure.
Just one injection will keep your system
pure. It will cure you of pride that puffs you
up and you start to trust in God and not in
luck!

As to your family, whether twelve or one,
this serum lets God's will be done.
Have you had your shot of Jesus' blood?
Until you do, continue to suffer sin's awful
flood.

LIFE INSURANCE

May I tell you of a life insurance?

It's of the highest grade.

Don't worry about the premium.
For the cost has already been paid!

For the loss of your eyes that see nothing
but evil and awful corruptions;
they will be replaced with better insight
that seeks to find goodness in others.

For the loss of those ears that hear rumors,
hearsay, or bad gossip -
replaced with those ears that delight to hear
The Gospel and praises of worship!

For the loss of both hands, quick to shed
blood and develops evil devices –
replaced with hands of comfort and ease
and soothing in every crisis.

Those feet that are quick to tread
unrighteousness and walk in the ways of

iniquity -will be replaced with feet that walk
in the path of holy purity.

I highly recommend this insurance:
The company never had any strife;
and although you get many benefits
It also guarantees new life.

MY CHRISTMAS GIFT

I received some wonderful Christmas gifts
and I have a large collection.

I don't think money was an object
in making my selections.

I believe the time and patience spent
must have taken quite a while.
And when I took my gifts,
I thought, "I must be a favorite child. "

My father gave me a gift of strength:
He taught me to be strong;
to never look down in defeat and never give
right for wrong.

My mother's gift was priceless:
Hers was the gift of love, patience,
gentleness, and meekness.
I believe hers came from above.

Her next gift was the time she sat
and taught me day by day.
Then she'd take my hands then kneel,

and showed me how to pray.

My brother's gift was showing me how to
gain respect
and still have decent, honest fun
without premarital sex!

My sister's gift was helping me see how my
future mate should be:
chaste, modest, loving and a life of purity.

My Sunday School teacher's gift to me
was teaching me the old three 'R's:
Repentance, Religion, Righteousness,
and to escape Satan's horrors.

My Pastor, the principal of this school -
his gift was the words of life.
He taught me I couldn't even spell
Christmas, without first spelling Christ.

After all those wonderful gifts to me,
my choice wasn't very hard.
You see, I too, gave a Christmas gift -
I gave my heart to God!

A SINNER'S PLEA

Oh God, my time has come to go
but I'm not ready to die.

All my sinful, wicked life is passing,
all before my eyes!

There goes the time, when I thought
I was having so much fun.
Time was mine to use my way.
My life had just begun.

There goes the time I did all those crimes.
I refused to take the blame.

There goes the crowd I hung out with
and took God's name in vain.

Oh! Please don't let me see the man
that bears my scars on his face;
inflicted when He tried to tell me about your
saving grace.

There's the time mother begged me, "Just
kneel down," while she prayed.
And oh, how I pushed her hand away

and happily went on my way!

Oh, Satan, you said my deeds were hid
and I should never doubt.
Now, too late, I find you're a liar
for my sins have been found out!

There goes the day I rejected Christ!
Oh, how my heart was hardened.
I would not hear his pleading voice
and would not accept His pardon.

Where are the many friends I had
that said they would always be true?
And Satan, who I served so well;
why, he's deserted me too!

Oh God, spare me, spare me, I pray.
I didn't know I'd be called soon.
I thought death came to older folks -
until he was in my room.

Now, I'm doomed to eternal hell
to be where eternity rolls.
The time has come for me to die!
and it is not well with my SOUL!

COMPANY

See who's knocking at my door!
I wonder who it can be.
I really don't feel like nobody visiting me!

Oh! Oh, I... well, Hello!
Lord, where did you come from?
Please excuse my condition.
You caught me clean undone.

I meant to keep my house in order.
Mary! Bring me that broom.
I knew you were coming back one day
but I didn't expect you this soon!

I'll clean those Playboy's off the chair
in case you'd like to sit down.
I'm only reading them because
my Bible can't be found!

Johnny, take those beer cans
and also that cigarette pack.
Take those decks of cards from where
My Sunday School book is at!

I gave the kids a little party last night.

It was small and nothing great.

I didn't wake them for Sunday School today
because they were up pretty late.

My husband, he works the night shift
and don't get home until ten.

That man going out the back door?
He's just a family friend!

No, these scars on my face and hands
didn't come from daily hard labor:
I was trying to prove some hearsay
and had a fight with my neighbor!

Lord, I don't have any Gospel songs.
I don't know when I've prayed.
No, I haven't won a soul for you.
Well, uh, no one knows I'm saved!

Lord, I meant to be ready for you;
meant to have my heart in tune.

Lord, I beg you, have me excused.
I didn't know you were coming so soon!

THANK GOD FOR THE DEVIL

Do you think that now you're free from sin?
You should relax and be at ease;
settle back on your religion,
and stop getting on your knees?

How do you read your Bible:
just the customary way
and quickly pick up a novel
and read the day away?

Your friend is living a wicked life.
Sin spins him with dizziness.
Do you help him forsake his ways;
or say, "It's not my business"?

Well, Christian friend, if this is your case,
you have sunk to another level.
For you have reasons to remain on your
knees
and thank God for the devil.

It's the devil that makes you dismiss God's
Word;
makes you think one verse is enough.

But, you recall, your soul needs that word!
And your Bible replaces other bad stuff.

It's the devil that says don't talk to your friends -
as in sin, they sink deeper and deeper.
But, how quickly to them you should go.
You are, after all, your brother's own keeper.

It's Satan that keeps you home from the church, giving what seems a good reason.
But you read where it says "assemble yourselves" and obey in and out of each season.

So, we'll even thank God for allowing Satan to try and lead us astray.
For the more that he tries, the more we defy by continuing to trust and obey!

AN OLD MAN'S MEMORIES

Just sitting here watching as the folks go by;
hearing them talk; listening to them lie!

Seems like they don't believe in God no
more.
My, what a pity!

It ain't just the worldly folks causing shame.
It's the ones who claim Jesus' Name.

Can't understand their religion!
Went down to hear the choir rehearse.
So full of pride, they might just burst.
They sing from the mouth, no heart!

The preacher got up and told his host.
They're ain't no such thing as the Holy
Ghost!
We'll, no need to think about him.

There was the deacon, praying loud as life -
just got through kissing the preacher's wife!
Did he ever hear of judgment?

They sing, 'Precious Lord Take My Hand'

and refuse to shake with their fellow man!
How can they love God they never seen -
these modern churches, with seats like
skin?

And everything's covered, including sin!
Not like the little church on the hill.
Now, you ask them for a good revival.
They'll wonder how you ever survived.
You're not like them I guess.

Well, this old religion I got, just fine.
Had it so long, I've lost track of time;
brought me safe so far.

BIBLE SCHOOL IS OVER

Bible school is over.
The books are put away.
Some of the teachers will soon depart
and some of them will stay.

Into the church we softly came,
looking bright and neat
to learn about the love of God
as we sit at the teachers' feet.

Bowing our heads, we learned to pray
just as children should -
asking God to help us
to be kind and true and good.

Lifting our voices in joyful hymns.
Oh! what a celebration!
I think the Angels joined in with us
as we sang of God's salvation.

Each day we learned of something new
as we studied God's Holy Bible.
Then we played such wonderful games.
Oh, not a moment was idle!

Swiftly, you went to your classes.
That showed you were anxious to learn;
willing and eager and trying so hard
to win those little gold stars!

Bringing those little children to Christ
is our most sacred job.
Just to feed and clothe them isn't enough.
We're supposed to train them for God!

NO WEAPON

I lost the battle I fought today
because I had no sword.

I left my 'lamp' that lights my path
so I stumbled on the road.

I couldn't prove that I'm an heir
when questioned by my rival.

I lost my chance to win a soul
because I left my Bible!

The war is on, the call gone out
for volunteers to enlist.
It's a people's war, not just about
the call for men to resist.

We uncover sin on every side
and fighting in every form.
The call is for men who won't compromise
nor be afraid of bodily harm.

Not all who enlist have the same role.
Some follow, while others will lead.

You must obey and do as you're told and
serve wherever the need.

You can expect hate and scorn.
Your friends will desert you too.
And criticism will feel like thorns,
but to your vow, you must always be true.

Before you enlist, you should pay the cost
and see if you're willing to pay.
You'll be hated for the stand you take
and you may lose your life on the way.

Are you willing to give up family;
the way you're accustomed to living?
If you enlist, your life will be one of
constantly fighting and giving.

You can be used as a leader.
You'll have a job on your shoulder.
But stand for the truth, whatever the price
and let each try make you firmer.

This Captain that you are serving Is a very
peculiar man.
The way He leads may be difficult
and you may not understand.

You may think you won't make a good soldier.
You may think Him you'll not pleased.
Well listen, just stand tall for your captain.
Then soldier, stay on your knees.

THEY JUST WENT ON AHEAD
(On the death of preachers)

Blessed are the dead that die in the Lord.

Comfort yourselves with these words:
The time has passed, memories go on,
and time cannot your thoughts disturb.

Riches, glory, and honor on earth,
you could never, never compare
what joy and peace that passes all else,
He will have with God up there.

Oh, that men would praise the Lord
for His mercies endure forever.

He had a oneness and fellowship with God
that not even death could sever.

A man of sorrow and acquainted with grief;
Our Lord understands your sorrows.
But rejoice, and again I say, rejoice

for you will clap hands on that great
tomorrow!

Death has no terrors, for the blood bought
one.
He gladly went on his way -
changing a world of darkness and pain
for a perfect, endless day.

"Abide with me" was his prayer to God.
He relied on Him through life.
He knew his God would always keep his very
precious life.

"Make me a blessing" must have been his
slogan,
for he went through life doing good.
Regardless of what others have did,
for the truth he has always stood.

Seeking heaven with eyes of faith,
he saw the doors open wide, not just ajar;
and the glories he saw on the other side
Was well worth dying for.

APPLYING FOR A HOME

Are you looking for a better home?
I know of some that are very pretty.
No, they are not located here;
but in a place called Celestial City!

You first must answer some questions
to see if you qualify
because there are conditions to be met
before you say "I'll try."

Let me try to describe these wonderful
homes:
First, they're on streets of gold!
I could never give a perfect description
because the half has never been told.
Now, the walls are made of Jasper.
The atmosphere is rare.
You won't have to fear the darkness
for, I'm told, there's no night up there.

The land Lord is Omnipotent -
so full of love and grace.
He explains everything in detail
when you see Him face to face.

The best part about those wonderful homes
is that the purchase has been made.
The land Lord so loved His tenants;
the price He gladly paid!

In order to live in these lovely homes,
you must give up the way you're living.
He doesn't force you to accept His terms.
He only asks if you're willing.

In this great Celestial City
there are no liars and gossip hunger;
no adulterers or fornication,
especially, no scandal mongers.

Everyone that lives in these homes
are full of love, joy, and peace.
There are no tears, sorrow, or pain
and happiness will never cease.

Now, while you are living here in this
"house," you have trouble and may even cry.
But just be patient and always be ready
until you are called to "Come, occupy."

GOING HOME

Evening has cast its shadows.
The birds have gone to rest.
Night has settled upon us
and the sun has sunk in the West.

Visions of glorious things
took the place of reality;
and then a restless urge to be
with immortality!

Even the angels watched in dawn
as another took off alone -
winging his way with the speed of light
to bring back one of their own.

Rolling the soft clouds to one side,
nothing could hide their view
of the heavenly host that watched to see
how quietly this one was brought through.

Angels have gotten a mansion ready,
and have waited breathlessly for the
heavenly messenger's return.
What a home coming that will be!
Standing there in front of the host

with His face aglow with smiles.
With loving arms opened wide
stands the Father to welcome His child!

Many friends and dear ones were made
and oh, they were dear to the heart.
And when whispers came 'soft and low,'
they knew it was time to depart.

We watch and see life
as it passes away;
and then when it's us,
Death takes no delay!

Down at Calvary, long ago,
the price to glory was paid.
And now with nothing to do but go,
we will find the welcome mat laid.

PECULIAR PEOPLE

The world can't understand us.
Some folks think we're crazy.
The way we act, the things we do,
makes them think our minds are hazy.

While they go to entertainments
and dance the newest lurch,
we gather our Bibles and hymn books
and gladly go off to church!

When they scorn and say things about us,
we act like we don't care:
even when shunned for doing right,
we just take them to God in prayer.

When slapped on one side of the face,
we simply turn the other cheek.
For us to stand and not defend ourselves
makes us appear cowards and weak.

They wonder what kind of people we are
who rejoice in the midst of depression;
and what kind of teenager who prefers
church to a rocking, rapping, jazz session.

They look wide eyed at our clothes and ask,
"How do you keep cool?"

And when our little ones should be at rest,
we have them going to Sunday school!

The beautiful girl who sings in the choir,
they see she's not making big money;
not making records in fancy nightclubs -
wasting her talent in church is so funny.

They wonder how that good looking
preacher
can be so set against sin!
Don't he know that eating bad fruit is the
new way of making cool friends?

Yes, we are peculiar people!
And we know they don't understand us.
But we have learned that precious secret
that keeps us free from the world and its
lust.

THE VERDICT IS YOURS

The world is a court room, and we are on
trial.
We can expect a vigorous offense
and we will need someone to represent us.

How good is your defense?
You have a lawyer, named Satan!
Well, I know he's defended a host,
but I have a famous attorney.
They call Him the Holy Ghost!

Your lawyer, you are considering,
I've heard he's crafty and sly:
he'll get your hopes up, and then sell you out
and leave you, sentenced to die!

"What of the Holy Ghost?" you ask.
Well, I know he's honest and true.
He'll stand by you when your trial is hard
and he will see you all the way through!

Your lawyer will keep you in his debt
by putting his price through the ceiling.
He will tell you, "Defense comes high!"
And you will start lying and stealing.

The lawyer who represents me
Has a solid foundation He laid;
And my only fee is believing in Him,
for all my debt has been paid!

I don't wonder if He is experienced.
I don't have to give depositions.
He heard my plea. He intercedes for me,
for He knows my every intention.

Yes, your lawyer has a very large practice -
clients here and far away.
But the folks he's tricked and put in despair -
they have forgotten how even to pray.

I've told you some things your lawyer will do.
He has ruined his clients by score.

For the sake of your life, make the right
choice.
Dear friends, the verdict is yours!

TO THE MAN OF GOD

Righteousness exalts a nation.
Sin is a reproach to any people.
Thank God for a man who's not afraid
to shout God's truth from a steeple.

Every nation has a 'voice'
crying in the wilderness,
calling all to repentance
and you were one of His best!

"Verily, verily, I say unto you,
you must be born again",
is the only topic of conversation
you have for the sinning man.

Salvation and the Savior's love
are the standards by which you abide.
And a woman whose price is far above
rubies is your companion by your side.

Winning souls for your precious Lord
is your only sacred job:
telling men to leave sin's road,
and be reconciled to God.
Knowing no race, color, or creed,

you came as a "sinner seeker",
for you have learned, by the grace of God,
that you are your brother's keeper.

Taking the name of Jesus with you,
you enter every fight.
Though often cast down, you never lose,
for the God of war is your might.

Eternal life in your Father's house
is the prize you're striving for.
To hear Him say 'well done'
Is what He'll say at the bar.

Telling a dying world about Christ
is your daily occupation:
Seeking ways and means whereby
you can tell His love to the nations.

NAME BRAND

When you go to the grocery store
to get a bar of soap,
you don't just pick any kind;
but a bar that's 'famous,' I hope.

Then when we go to the butcher shop,
here, too, we want the best.
So we search until we find the label
of the kind we need not guess.

You go to a fancy dress shop,
and there you spend some time
because you want to be sure the designer
is the best one of her kind.

Remember the time that you got sick?
Only the best doctor would do.
And even if your money is slim
you want the best brand of shoe.

Well, if you're seeking salvation,
not just any religion will do.
There's only one that meets every need
and it has a name brand too!

This salvation that I recommend
is won by the name of "Jesus".
He's food and clothing and medicine
and from every sin, He frees us.

This salvation of Jesus
will clean the dirtiest heart.
He'll clean your thoughts and your mind,
and give you a brand new start!

And this great "name brand', salvation
will feed your starving soul.
Just feed upon His word each day
because it's good for young and old.

This Jesus is a doctor
that can heal the heart of man,
remove your thoughts from evil,
and make you whole again.

So if you're looking for a good salvation
this brand may not be the rave.
But it's the only name under heaven
whereby a man can be truly saved!

HELP WANTED - WOMEN ONLY

Wanted: young women to model.

You can be *plain or fair.*

If willing, you will be paid to show
what the well-dressed woman should wear.

First, a change will have to be made.
Yes, there's a rule that has a price.
You must be willing to present your bodies
as a living sacrifice.

Now, let's remove the lipstick.
Now, your face looks sweeter.

Next, the red and fancy finger nails
that make your hands look neater.

Let's take that deep V from your dress.
A simple V won't make you smother.

Now, take those pants that are much too
tight, and give them back to your brother!

Next, pull off those indecent shorts.

You may have to use a knife.
"Naked you came into the world"
Don't mean you go naked through life!

Ladies, you must live a holy life.
You have a serious job!
These children didn't just happen to appear.
They were sent to you from God!

Don't try to compete with men.
Leave their affairs alone.
The kind of men that rule the world
are the boys you train at home.

Ladies, those girls you are training
will someday be mothers too.
So teach them to be honest and chaste -
Remember, they are watching you!

Yes, you have reached the joy of your life.
Keep the peace of God on your face.
Let everything you say and do come from a
heart of grace.

To all the ladies who answer this ad -
you're working together as one;

and after doing your best at the end of the day,
Your Master will say "well done!"

THE BIG PARTY

The house was decorated so beautifully.
Everything was all in place.
The waiter and the butler had come on time,
and oh, the wine was chilled to taste!

The piano was really in tune.
The band would be very hot.
They would dance the wax off the floor,
yes, tonight this was the spot!

"Hi, Willie, you are the first one here,
and boy, are we going to chase the blues!"
"Yes," said Willie, "well come sit down
'cause man, I got some news.
That big band you were looking for -
you should hear what they were playing:
something about Amazing Grace,
tears were falling, but none were swaying!"

"But, Willie, did you see, Joe Henry?
He was bringing his brand new sax."

"Oh, yeah," said Willie, "I saw him
downtown.
Man, he was there passing out tracts!

Remember the girls who were together?"

"Yes, one of their voice was hoarse."

"Well, count them out too, 'cause from now
on they are singing in a gospel chorus!
Wait 'til you hear bout Fred, the life of the
party.
He had a Bible - man, the biggest I've seen!
With some kids on his front steps, all with
hands up
teaching them - uh, John 3:16!
I stood around listening for awhile
until he said something I don't understand.
He said, 'if you want eternal life,
You must be born again!'"

"Hey man, what are you putting the lights
out for? The party ain't even begun!"

"Man, I want to be born again
and I'm going to see how it's done!"

THE VICTIM RAP SONG

See that cute loveable baby -
Innocent and sweet as a beautiful daisy?
Mom and Dad treat him so tender.
They plan and say, "He'll be a big spender!"

So they treat him as a special model:
pampering, humoring, how they coddle!

"We will teach him how to play cards," says Mom.
"Why sure," says Dad, "cards are no harm!"
"Go get me some cigarettes, only son."
"Mamma, Daddy, can I have one?"
"Oh, let him try, and see how it's done!"
Mom misses money belonging to them.
Dad says, "Now, don't fuss and embarrass him! He needs money, like Bob and Tim!"
Mom questions Dad, about his actions.
Dad answers her to her satisfaction.
The boy knows better, but sees her reaction!

It gets too hot for parents to wear clothes
So they walk about with bodies exposed:
no modesty, no shame, even when they repose!

Dad says, "Sundays are good as any time
for fun and games of any kind;
and the boy can get religion later down the
line!"

The child never sees his parents together in
prayer;
never sees a Bible around...anywhere!
But he often hears Mom and Dad curse and
swear!

All the way up to a young adult age,
the child does nothing but sin and rage!
He grew up, an angry protestor;
so now he's jailed: a serial molester!

Are you making a victim of your child,
as he trusts you with his loving smile?
He was put in your keeping for a little while.
You will answer to God, for your parenting
style!

The Journey Continues

Writings of Edward Blair
*****

JOB

Job,
a tool of Satan he became -
if he would blaspheme God's good name.

Satan, wanted God, to let him go
to cause Job boils from head to toe!

So God permitted him one try:
"Touch his body, but he must not die!"

Satan laughed with untold glee:
"To think, that God could outfox *me*!"

He struck good Job, one clear night
while he was standing for all that's right.
The boils appeared with sudden horror;
Job would scream for no tomorrows!

His wife of years would wail and cry:
"Why not curse God and die?"

In pain, Job raised his head to say,
while he attempted hard to pray,
"No other friend have I in this world - One
who is greater than the richest pearl!
There is a difference between God and
venom.
You talk like one of the foolish women!

Naked I came. Naked I'll go.
This one thing, I'll always know -
The devil is a liar.
He lost God's best.
Praise the name of God; give me more of
the test!"

JUDAS

Of all the men who walked with him
of thousands in the land,
The Son of God, in earthly form,
gave a chance to this unworthy man.

What breeds in us, this kind of being,
to have a right at special dreams
and cast away the human side
while shutting out the Holy beams?

The Master raised the dead and healed;
gave life to all He would;
fed thousands on a hilly slope;
forgave our sins, because He could!

Envy, greed - we know not what
that planted a traitor's kiss.
This He felt, with all his heart,
was felt more than the soldier's fist.

The traitor shared His Master's meal -
His last on earth to eat.
Then went he and collected thirty coins,
and "true love" met its first defeat!

Beware of kisses given often.
Understand what underneath may lie,
for Judas kissed Him on Friday,
and later, others watched Him die!

Of all the names mothers give their sons;
for kings, statesmen such as that,
the universe shuns, creation hates
any called Judas Iscariot!

LAZARUS

In the darkened tomb, he waits
for the long awaited call;
sustained by faith and courage,
because the promise is for all.

It's cold and damp and murky
in this place where deadness lives.
But he knows a call is coming.
So he waits with anxious thrill.

Others lay beside him
in this tomb of carved-out stone.
Then... his grave clothes started falling
and he waits to see his own!

Suddenly, he hears it!
His name... like called in court!
Four days late, but He made it.
"Lazarus! Come forth!"

The sunshine felt so very clean.
His skin did radiate.
His friend had called his name alone,
lest others would not wait!

The Master once had said, "believe"
in truth, He did imply; for death is no victor,
when God knows your name.
In Him, you just sleep... never die!

MARY

Pitiful she is to view:
falling, stumbling, ragged too;
crying, foaming, mouth in rage...
Demons tearing at her awful gaze.

She screamed so loud, it caused a shudder;
Rolling, crawling, in a filthy gutter.

"Someone do something with this thing!
She spoils our praying and attempts to
sing."

Possessed by demons, in numbers... legion;
and only 'One' could see the reason.

He took her softly by her arms and said,
"Demons out! Be gone!"

They tried to make her spirit doubt,
but the voice of God drove the demons out.

Her eyes grew clear, her face brand new,
and Jesus said "That's what faith will do."

When the cross was over, buried He lay.
All had left Him for another day.
There was one who stayed at the grave yard
scene - the one that demons left –
Mary Magdalene!

THE CROWN

Chosen for its pain

Designed to pierce the brain

Ugly in its shape

It spelled the victim's fate.

Twisted, to match our hearts
with its shiny pointed darts

Made into a crown

Not placed... but shoved hard down!

Onto a tender head
whose skin so easy bled
and blood dripped into the eyes,
that hours later died.

Crowns are made for regal folk -
Kings: designed for life -

This blooded head all bruised and bowed
was one who died in strife.

Perhaps the thorns will change
by some miracle of chance.
Then this head which hung in shame,
will lead the Victors' dance.

STILL, I MISS YOU
(My Mother's Absence)

It's been over nine long years
when last I saw you smile.

A frozen mask, a stillness strange,
hid your eyes, from me, your child.

I think about you often,
there beyond the gaze of upward sky.

I try to see beyond the stars
to see if, truly, you can fly!

I'm stuck at times with living here -
this awesome task of being.

I wish that you and I could speak
and worlds not cloud our hearing;
encouraging one another like we used to,
discussing great spiritual matters.

We would drink coffee - black, and tea;
grow happy, joyful, then much sadder!

What's heaven like, Mother?
Is there room for one more?
Can I visit on occasion?
Would you describe its decor?

I still miss the quiet talks,
the profound questions you always asked.
You know the answers better now
as the years up there have passed!

CARESS

Hold me soft and tender, near.
Erase my doubts, banish my fear.
Caress me in your arms so lite.
Arrange my dreams, and make them
alright!

When I'm alone, my heart repeats
its cadence slowly in its hurried beats
of desperate pleas for hands to hold,
of arms to brace against the cold!

Caress my brow when furrows glide
as if some crooked path to ride.

Embrace the lips that quiver soft.
End my bitter evening frost.

Caress the hands that seek their mate.
Assign you love to seal my fate.

Caress, caress, caress me now.
Then take my heart, and show me how!

MY CUSHION

Of all the things you are to me,
the one that keeps me pushing
is when I'm feeling lost and scared
and your arms become my cushion.

A cushion is a place of rest,
a moment to feel at ease.

You give to me such simple peace
and a cautious, wanting tease.

Your body bears my pounds with care,
as a neck, its precious gems;
into your arms, I melt again,
then lose my strength of limps.

A cushion placed upon my bed;
a cushion in my arms;
a quiet place of sleep and dreams
where a cushion gives its charms!

HERS

The poems she wrote were heartfelt gems,
the kind that only suffering brings.
She saw in them joy and faith, and knew that
she could forever dream.

Life for her was viewed through motherhood
and prayer, the bended knee, and tear-filled
air.

In poetry, she could direct her praise to a
God she never saw, but she could rhyme and
place His name where all others stood in
awe.

She watched her life unfold through
hardened hands of motherhood.
And by candle dim on darkened nights, she
wrote so others knew where her faith stood.

The God she loved so much on earth is now
her constant friend.
He has written a poem for her, whose lyrics
to chase eternity.
And she, like them, will never end!

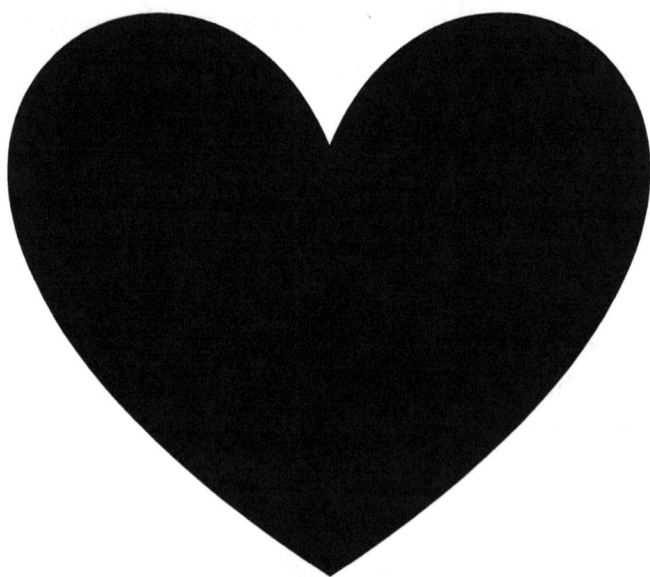

MY DAUGHTER'S HAND
(My Foster Daughter, Bubble)

Walking her to Head Start school, my
thoughts were business driven.

She skipped, jumped, and ran ahead as if life
was newly given.

She spoke in childish prattle quickly:
her words, to me, made little meaning.

I had done this ritual so many times, its
meaning, nothing new; until one day, she
held my hand and I suddenly felt her hands
too!

It was the soft and trusting touch
she conveyed with so much pride
that she was walking to her school
with her hero by her side.

I felt a tender nerve in me send signals to my
brain
which said, in clear, distinctive thought -
school walks would never be the same.

I watch her now as she jumps along, heading to her schoolhouse door.
I hold all nature still at bay, for I must hold her hand some more.

CALVARY

A hill for centuries which knew no cheer
was made even worse when it met the
spear.

A place where men who sinned should cry;
a place where, now, God's Son did die!
Calvary - the clouds now cover

Two men punished, who deserved each
other.

A third placed center… innocent too,
hung on a cross for me and you.

A crowd had gathered, shouting mad:
"He lied," they said, "he did all things bad!"

"Come down, healer man, can't you fight?"

He couldn't. The spikes held much too
tight.

Calvary - a hill, a place, a date
Infamous for its victim's fate.

One thief cried, "You over there, save me too!"

"No," cried the other, "we are guilty for what we do!"

The only answer for this sin-cursed world was on Calvary's hill - a precious pearl - who hung His head, died in shame.

Now Calvary's hill finally has its fame!

MY MOTHER'S BED
(When in Despair)

Sometimes my nights are restless,
devoid of sleep or ease.

The quietness that others have
would not come, if I said, "Please!"

I toss and turn all night throwing covers in
all directions.

My pillow's drenched and wrinkled
and my dreams have lost protection.

I recall my years when younger as a child at
Mommy's feet when fears were my
companion.
Only she could bring relief.

I would crawl into her big old bed where
she slept at night,
and the terrors, dangers, and all the pain
would magically take flight.

Perhaps it was the softness of the spot in
which she lay.

Perhaps it was her body's scent
that only mothers have who pray!

Whatever magic that sleep did have -
perhaps her old bedspread;
If I could spend one night again
in my mother's peaceful bed!

RUTH

Naomi left her husband's land
to seek for bread so they could stand
and try to keep the family pure
for they were Jews and were unsure
of how they all would survive the drought
and keep away the family's doubt
of what God's plan for them would be
when their land was left besides the sea.

Her husband died, then her sons.
For her was nothing left to mourn.
There were two daughters from a cursed
land but married her sons, and now had no
man.

"Turn back", she cried, "leave me soon.
No more sons to leave my womb."

Oprah left Naomi, returning to her kin;
Ruth remained defiant, vowing never to
leave her again.

"Your home, my home," she cried with
delight.

"Your God, my God, with my sinful life."

Returning with Naomi, Ruth gleaned in the field.
She would pick fallen corn, rather than steal.

The rich man saw her, his passion enflamed,
He asked his helper, "Discover her name!"

Her name is Ruth, a Gentile denied. Yet
Boaz would make her his Gentile Bride.

What strange things happens in God's holy plan when a Gentile woman, from a wicked land,
Can be a part of hope and delight
and become an heir of the Lord Jesus Christ!!!!!!

MOODS

Pained expressions race across my brain.

Contorted feelings grasp in pain.

The moods come visibly, horribly clear

that something deep lies very near.

A mouth to speak, explain, inform,

can't find the words that need be born.

The moods still constantly inside my being

turning me, spinning me, nothing seeing.

Happy one minute, depressed the next;

joys beholding the broader context:

pushing out, inside my chest -

seeking escape from life's empty test.

Sad, crying, laughing, fearful,

singing, begging, anxious, cheerful -

this rush of moods that leave me dry.

That, when they're finished, leave only a

sigh!

SAMSON!

An Angel told a barren wife
that she would one day bring forth life -
a special child unlike before.

So drinks, libations, she began to pour!

The Angel warned that this child's life
would be lonely and filled with strife.

"A razor never must touch his head.
And wine, strong drink, he never must be
fed!"

A Nazarite under special vow;
his knee to others must never bow.

Strength to him of thousands given -
directed, and by the Spirit, driven!

A name was needed for one so handsome.
The Angel warned, "You must call him
Samson!"

He became a judge and helped his tribe.
Then his woman... she was paid a bribe!

"You must deceive him," they warned her
plain,
"Or your family will know such pain!"

Delilah was this beauty true
whose deceptive wiles, Samson never
knew!

She begged him, cried every night
to divulge the secret of his might!

He fooled her twice with funny lies
and she begged him more
until he could not deny!

"Cut my hair, my strength is gone.
God would leave, and I would be alone!"

He slept that night, his head in her lap,
forgetting, that love can be a trap!

They came, blinded him… prisoner caught!
Made him a clown of the baser sort!

While in the mill grinding flour,
He prayed that God would restore his
power.

His enemies needed him for games
in their drunken rage to shout his name!

Placing his hands between two stone walls:
"God, let me die, when this place falls!"

He killed more in death than in life.
His time on earth was play and strife!

His name was Samson.
Some never call great.
But God put his name in the Hall of Faith!

RESURRECTION VICTORY

For three long days
and three long nights
the tomb above remained an eerie sight.

Guards were posted who were straight and
tall -
defying any theft to mar His fall.

But it was out of view.

The battle really raged;
for here in hell's domain, nothing was ever
staged.

Whoever was there would always remain;
for here, life and death were not the same.

Jesus was different though, in all degrees,
for He created hell and the seas.

In awe, the demons shied away
from His majestic walk and sway!

He proclaimed the victory.

He was sent to win that man may never die
again!

The cross, he said, wasn't death, but a door;

He would leave first, then millions more!

Demons were angry, fearful, defeated;
Satan, defeated, defrocked and demented!

Count the days out loud:
one,
two,
three.

He is risen, for you and for me!

Victory!

Victory!

victory sweet!

The Master will never death repeat.

The sun, in its journey, hurries to rise

and change death's darkness into
resurrection's skies!

FROM A SOLDIER'S PERSPECTIVE

The wind is cold.
Storm clouds race across a darkened sky.
All is stillness, silence.

All eyes look up to see, to understand, to try
and feel.

Suddenly, a cry is uttered from a throat that
had been hit by a fist that had no heart.
A voice is heard from lips that have been
swollen by a hand to mock their truth.

This agony, this sight, this death of a body
drenched in sweat mixed with dried blood
upon which the flies are even fed;
thus even here He provides for His creation's
need.

His eyes are large, stained with strain and
fleeting sleep,
darkened by that hand again, which doesn't
count the times it strikes, only as many as is
needed.

Who is this emaciated prisoner, stretched like a tent across a door, with nails so deep, they defy His movements?

Look at Him!!! Swollen, naked, dying…

"Wait."

He cries something

Oh! Nothing but "It's finished!"

MOSES

Called by God when a babe in the womb
to lead his enslaved people from a life of
doom

A handsome child, innocent as air
whose hatred Satan would not spare

Children born under three years' old
would lose their lives before they could
unfold.

So Moses was kept from Pharaoh's clutches
by being hidden in the Nile's bull rushes!

Divine protection kept his growth
until God performed for him His oath.

He would bring Israel's children out
and cross the desert by a chosen route!

Pharaoh withstood God; he never did beg.

So the Creator unleashed on him His
plagues!

Eleven times, Pharaoh's heart denied
until the last one came, all the first born
died!

"Out, out!" Egypt's king cursed and swore.
"Moses, your face I'll see no more!"

God led them out, scared as could be,
and placed their backs against the angry Red
Sea.

Behind, Pharaoh's army, bringing death;
in front, the Sea whose waves did quake!

"We should have stayed and died in Egypt!
Who wants this freedom, Moses you can
keep it!"

Moses cried out, "Lord, we're people of the
sod!"

And God said calmly, "Stretch out your rod."

When faced with danger, perils, and fear,
look for the cloud that God keeps near!

Moses found later, you do more with less

When you trust God's power in the wilderness!

THE VICTOR

He is called the Savior
because He paid the price
for goods completely tarnished and denied
not once, but thrice!

Interrogated for hours, made to stand
alone;
friends who traveled with Him left,
returning to their homes!

The crown of thorns was heavy, hurt with
pain when touched -
not the head on which it lay, but the soul it
scarred so much!

The spikes were long and rusty, made sharp
pointed at the end.
The sound would echo loudly as it parted
holy skin!

Stretched like awnings tightly on a cross of
wooden frame;
many wear its symbol because they cannot
love its shame!

"We won, we won!" the Devil said under the earth in hell.

Three days later, Heaven's turn, and God gave the Victor's Yell!

He is called the Savior because from Him, the flood of crimson, sanctifying, all-encompassing Blood!

THE WORD

Given before the universe was born, it sustains, transforms, the soul of man; restores the hopes of many who have lost their faith and simple way of living; provides the direction from which all may find their way back home.

It untangles doubt, confusion, and dismay; provides for clarity in order that I may not stray.

When soul and spirit collide in their fusions, each attempting to direct the will in its wayward aim, the Word interprets each one's essence and blends their focus in such a way that the glory is given to God's Holy name.

The name is the Word, whose flesh it once became and lived and died and rose again because it always has been the same.

THE TWELVE

Of all the men who history acclaims,
it's the band of twelve we least profane.

From backgrounds varied, sorted, and rare,
they were well chosen because each would
dare
to start a journey, unknown, untried,
whose end result was they all have died!

Fisherman, tax collector and a traitor too;
it was what they preached that made them
few.

At times they doubted, quarreled, and
fought;
but their Godly fear, was why they were
sought!

They were human people, like us all.
Unlike many, they were heavenly called.

All but one remained devoted
It was to money he was devoted!

Their master trained them very well.

They gave us a choice: heaven or hell.

Endowed with enablement and the Spirit's power,
they healed the sick and made demons cower.

History recalls it was not for themselves
that eleven made it, and only one did fail!

THE SON OF GOD

Angels watched with bated breath; the dawn
of the earth's twilight. For all the forces of
the universe were drawn in space and time;
led by a small star bright.

Who knows the way of transfixed life, the
coming together of being?

But He came, in simple, easy pain, with only
cattle seeing!

The animals' eyes were first to gaze upon the
hope of man. Their soft breaths were
covering for the future of the land.

With small hands grasping, pulling at the air,
cooing softly, warmly: "He," thinking
thoughts, "we must not dare!"
His birth was before the sunrise, before
creation's being. Yet, He's here in infancy
and before creation's seeing, existence,
birth, death, existing forever and a day.

Time was unknown, a memory, yet constant
as "the Way!"

There are many names to describe the awesomeness of Him. Yet simply put, "the Son of God," at that sound, the earth is thrilled!

THE KING WHO STAYED HOME

The night was sticky, humid, wet.
It caused his royal brow to sweat.

Up to the roof of his palace, high,
a place to view the starry sky;
a solitary empty space where kings can go,
without losing face and do what other
people do
when hot and tired and feeling blue.

She was bathing, washing in her yard.
He stopped praying to his Lord.
His eyes could not her figure leave
and his passion grew hotter than a Summer's
eve.

Setting aside all morals and right,
he commanded she come and spend the
night.
Informing Joab, his trusted captain,
to place her husband in front of the javelin.

The husband died, loving his king.
She was soon ready a baby to bring!

When God told Nathan, the mighty Seer,
"Go find David, whisper this in his ear:
'A man had one lamp, devoted and true.
Another man took it. King, what would you
do?'"

"Kill him!" cried David, slamming down his
hand.

Nathan said softly, "King, *you* are that man!"

Kings should lead armies into battles and
fights;
never stay home and watch starry nights!

WHEN HEARTS KNIT
(Jonathan and David)

Saul, angry, bitter, and sad,
hated his son for the friend he had.

Jonathan loved David, this sheep keeping
man, because he knew what faith could
stand.

David's family, poor and lowly,
knew, of course, that kings were holy.

They wished that David would remain -
a shepherd boy, devoid of fame.

But God has a way of breaking through
to alter plans, and fortunes, too!

So from following sheep in mire and dung
Until upon his head, a crown was worn!

Jonathan would slip outside at night.
Together, they watched the stars grow
bright.

They shared that time when their hearts
were blended, till Jonathan was wounded
and his life was ended.

Pain and sorrow can evoke such grief
that only a poem can bring relief;
So David wrote out Psalm 23
For times to come when it's you and me!

BODY COUNT

It's not the jungles of Nam I'm in.

The concrete ground is not Charlie's den.

The buildings high, glistening bright,
inform my senses there's no need to fight.

And yet my dreams reveal this truth
of the body count of today's black youth.

The body count I left over there
were soldiers too, both young and fair.

But this pointless, senseless killing spree
of teens so young was never meant to be.

Black bodies, brown bodies with pants that
sag - in a one-size-fits-all body bag.

The body count I thought I left behind
still cries for reason in my distorted mind.

A chalk outline is their only fame;
and they lose that too in the morning rain.

A body count here is on a playground yard where hopscotch and marbles should only be hard.

The young are competing for space in the grave and their breath dissipated as the bag covers their head.

Once inside, there's no freedom, no pride.

The body count bag has the zipper outside.

MY GRANDMOTHER'S QUILT

Years ago and summers past, when snow was falling in my town and the wind blew against all that moved.

The quilt was born!

I would walk in the snow as if in a daze. As the white flakes hit my nose and melted on my outstretched tongue, looking up, my vision became lost.

My laughter was loud.

The cold was welcomed.

The journey to my grandmother's house, wasn't far. It was a journey made like the ancient warriors as they searched for new adventures: always searching, never satisfied, always searching!

The distance to her house was made gladly only by my imagination.

Pulling up my collar against the wind, I pretended I was in a cave. Here I would remain until the winter passed. Oh well, I had to come out. Dreams end all too soon.

As she met me at her door, she scooped me up like some gigantic bird and rushed me to her fireplace.

"You'll freeze. You'll freeze," was her song to me.

She placed me in her bed so large, until space was lost on me.

"Settle down, my love, settle down," the next verse of her sung was sung.

Then she would cover me with her quilt. A quilt so large, it was as if it was hiding me from life. This quilt had squares woven in time and space.

As I lay underneath my heavenly quilt, I saw small rays of light shine through from the ceiling bulb. The warmth of the quilt caused me to weep.

How came these squares to be?

What pain had caused such labor, such determination to complete?

What memories produced these squares of life, interwoven together by colors and despair?

What theme held it together, that it provided so much warmth to the living?

Here's a square for Tommie, long since passed.

Then there's a square for Ann, her square when sisters clash.

There was Billie's square, her favorite son.

Last was Jan's square, who had no one.

My mother's square, why so black?

My father's square, why does it lack?

Susie's square was so pretty green.

Adam's square, was never to be seen.

So many squares, so many tales; so many squares, so many hells. All these squares done in God's great sun. Here's my square... why, it's not done.

MY IDOL
(The short comings of men)

He was gifted - a Black man,
defiant of all convention;
daring to be different,
easily going upstream against all currents.

This man was my idol.

His presence, as my teacher, made me aspire
to dream dreams out of reach, yet
believable, because he told me so.

He would teach science,
Math,
history,
all with knowledge far advanced beyond his
years.

A tall handsome man was he.

He was easily entreated.

With a haggard brow,
a woeful glance,
an embracing smile,

he seemed to like me, even my question-asking, information-seeking, inquisitional approach to things.

Yes, he was my idol.

He had but to speak,
and certainly waters would again part in two
and miracles would take place.

One day, he sat behind his desk at lunch.

The room was empty but for he and me.

He relaxed.

His foot, he put upon the desk without his shoe!

It was for me a crushing feeling,
a sickening sadness.

A god had fallen!

His sock had one big hole
and his greater toe was free!

I don't worship idols anymore,
because their falls are much too hard to
bear!

OLD GLORY

The wind blows my furls softly. A breeze stirs me to attention and urging me to once again remain watchful. I am Old Glory, your flag, your sentinel, the guardian of your shores! I sit atop the greatest places; adorn the most famous homes; drape the most esteemed of the fallen; presented to the weeping widows; lowered when the nation cries.

This is the nation I guard.

I launch ships, lead into battles, guide the parade of fools and nobles. I am spat upon, trampled by the non-caring, who have invested nothing; worn over the private parts of those whose allegiance is to vice, not victory.

And yet I still fly!!!!

But there is a part of me which cries out to surrender, not to enemies, but to guilt: not mine, but my nation's, for not only do I fly over grandeurs of beauty, I fly over the pain of broken dreams.

When you are sleep, I watch old men and old women, who once saluted me with pride, remove their meals from cans of trash and eat and die. I watch black and white, red and yellow, sleep not on beds of ease, but over sidewalk grates and cover themselves with steam.

The wind doesn't blow as hard at night, and I see secrets entered into by men who would sell your nation. I see husbands who love to fight, not their enemies, but those that bear their names. I see blood, once shed on shores of distant lands, now cover American hands!

REMEMBER

We've parted now, our own separate ways,
each seeking for something coming out of
our haze.

What do we do now?
It's over, it's done.

Simply try to recall the years of our fun.

Remember the time we promised our hearts
that we'd never leave because we were too
smart?

And we built our romance on promises
meant?

Remember our kisses, and frequent
attempts?

Remember the night I lost all your keys
and we laughed so loud, that we couldn't
breathe?

We found them; of course, they never were
missing.

It was my way of touching you, searching you… kissing.

Remember the cake? It was your first try of playing housewife; oh yes, the chicken you fried!

I loved it, of course, I had no choice. And we patted our stomachs as we ate and rejoiced.

Remember you whispered, "him, you'd never forget?"

The tension so tight; I rubbed your waist to your neck.

My arms encircled you, slowly and soft; and memories of him, gradually lost!

What happened to us?

What ended our chance of becoming real people, in a lovers' romance?

Recall all the memories, of days in September, which only leave now the things to remember.

MY NAME IS DEATH

Cold, without respect, my name is Death.

I claim; I don't redeem.

My name is Death, and all come under my sway.

Youth fail to see their end.

The old wish me away.

Young girls lose the luster of their charms.

Young men never see their offspring.

My name is Death, and I appear when you don't invite me. My warning and my end both arrive together!

In pain, some beg for me.
In grief I thrive.
In despair, I revel.
In life, I flee.

Some claim they have escaped my clutch by a "near death episode," but when they awaken, I'm there again.

This time for real.
I give no second chances.
My name is Death.

Fear is my play field; anger, my friend; rage, my wife.

My domain isn't a cold, damp ground, covered with crooked crosses and unkempt grass, where spirits play at night and yell "boo!"

I live in hearts that have no purpose: where light refuses to shine, where hatred sits enthroned, and jealousy is king.

My name is Death.
You know you've seen me.
You don't understand me.
I am a door. Where it leads, only life determines.

My name is Death.

MY ATTEMPT AT
RHYME AND PROSE

I wrote a poem.
It went like this:
Complete in all my dreams,
Searching constantly for themes,
Never finding what it means
To make a poem, I feel supreme.

Prose goes like this:
Yesterday left me with feelings uneasy and surreal; perhaps all my yesterdays were only feelings, caused by time and chance.
So the writer writes, and writes the substance only what he believes it to be. For rhyme and prose are only arrows dispatched by the same hand, launching into whatever target heart is open!

MY NAME IS LOVE

I'm not bought in bunches of reds, yellows or blues.

My name is Love, and I'm not bought in 5-10 or 12 pound boxes that put calories on your kitchen scale.

My name is Love, and I'm not put on dollar-twenty-five cent cards with manufactured sayings on their back.

My name is Love, and I don't consist of trinkets, beads or odors.

My name is Love, and I come home after 8-9 hours, tired and resentful, and find dinner, bath, and bed ready!

My name is Love, and I come home from 10-11 hours, angry, pushy and blaming and find dinner, bath and bed ready.

My name is Love, and I come home after rain, traffic, wet and find dinner, bath and bed ready.

Of all the things which make me inspire the reds, yellows and blues, the 5-10 and 12 pound boxes and the manufactured sayings, this is what I am:
I'm always consistent. I am always available. My name is Love. I am there when grief is present; joy is full; depression is near; when death gives the illusion of winning.

My name is Love, and what matters is not that you know me, but that you never define me... simply allow me!

THE MARKET BLOCK

"Up on the block!"
Hands that pull, pry, paw and push,
delighting themselves over every inch of my
flesh.

"Who will give me 8?" a thousand eyes
pierce my privacy, holding it up for all to see.
The on-looking women's faces turn red. The
men whisper to each other.

"Who will give me 10?"
I stand on one foot. It's hard because the
shackles don't allow it.

"Dance!" How? The music I hear has no
beat.

"Who will give me 20?"

"Open your mouth!" A finger, rude, runs its
course over my ivory teeth: pull my joys,
pinches my lips.
"Big, aren't they?"

"Who will give me 25?"

"Bend over!" Something inside me resisted;
the shame engulfed me.
Who am I? What am I?
"What is its name?"

"Whatever you want it to be."
Tears began to fall, not from the pain of the
hurt, but because no one knew my name.
My sense of self was lost, left on the sand a
million years ago!

"Who will give me 30?"
"It's a good price, it's been paid before."
"SOLD!!!!!!!!"

As I came down from the block, I saw
another generation coming up. I whispered
to her as she passed by, trembling:
"They may feel all but your spirit; they may
buy all but your pride. Come down from that
block and stay alive!!!"

ELEGY ON A MONUMENT

Cast in Black marble,
It silently sits
Bearing the names
Of all who were hit.

Quietly watching,
Bearing thousands of marks;
Displaying the stories
Of non-beating hearts.

Memoirs of names,
Hopes, cast in lines;
Detailing the exploits
Of the shot and the mined.

Here, there's a brother;
There, an uncle, a friend.
A father, a lover,
An adventure's sad end.

There are places for dreamers,
Places for calm.
This sacred shrine
Is for the heroes of "Nam."

A constant reminder
Of a nation's debate
When it gave up its sons
Because it made a mistake.

When it rains, I'm the saddest, because
that's when I pray
That their names on the stone, will not
wash away.

THE CRUISE SHIP
(The unwanted voyage)

They marched, like dead men together.

A chain of iron from neck to blackened neck,
cutting into yellows, brown, old, and young
skins, caused the blood to give their bodies a
reddish stain.

Slowly they marched.

No songs existed, as earlier in the camp,
where music was the praise to long dead
gods and hoped-for tomorrows; where joy
was sitting with one's family, friends, lovers,
and counting dreams each dared to share.

Their trail was made by the lash of the whip,
which, every time it kissed their backs, sang
its own song and left its lyrics for centuries
to come. The dead must be dragged along,
because time was the enemy and who could
spend money not in pocket.

"Hurry aboard...cast off...set sail!"

Stored below because the sun, so used to most, must not become familiar for a while. Head to head, breath to breath, touching places once forbidden, now community for all.

See the swollen wrists, ankles, necks; vomit, green and yellow, sometimes the color of the prey they had to eat.

Above, the women gave in to force, by one, by two, who cares to count.

Then the sound of the splash: "next!"

A brave one escapes the hole, stood atop the deck, and decided that the sharks, which swam beside the floating casket, were more noble company than the beasts who looked like he.

It arrived: this floating grave, manned by those whose only thought was for the gain it carried, not the agony it caused.

And from below came up Africa's seed to spread and ripen, and perhaps, just perhaps, remember the ship upon which they came....... and those who died on a cruise of shame.

AN EGG WITH NO SPERM
(For a daughter who never had a father)

How strange it seems to me
to have never known your pedigree
and then to be without descent,
never knowing what a father meant!

To come along in passion's heat:
a flurry of sweaty arms and feet;
a product of a high pitched sigh;
and glad she never slides down their thighs.

To see other eggs with well-known sperms
and you feel at times like a hated germ.

How strange it seems to me
to never have known your pedigree.
I saw my daughter (whose mine, she's not)
for I was not there, when emotions were
hot.
Who, while in school, watched other eggs
kiss their real sperms with delightful bliss!

When I dropped her at the schoolhouse
door, she grabbed me tight, like never
before.

She gazed in my eyes for permission to be -
the start of her paternity.

I held her close, like other sperms I saw;
kissed her forehead, and felt her thaw.

How delightful,
now it seems to me
that she finally has a branch
in a family tree.

MY NAME IS FEAR

My name is Fear, and I am king!

I claim that title because all pay homage to me.

My reach is far, extending from the lowliest of life to the highest, for even they tremble at my approach!

My name is Fear, and all respond to me.

Power is conceded to me; joy is willed to me; dreams are deferred to me; and expectancy is delayed by me.

My name is Fear.

I make the strong quiver as if bow strings were their sinews; the weak I give no chance; and the brave rethink themselves.

My name is Fear, and I have caused the masses to act as one without thought; the mighty to seek relief from their falls from high places; and the young to wonder why they don't succeed.

My name is Fear.

I act out of context and misperception and no faith for my weapons. With no context, all is failure.

With no perception, all things are wrong; with no faith, who can stand?

My name is Fear, and I cause brave men to re-think themselves; ideas of substance to disintegrate; relationships to fail. I set black against white, yellow against brown, brown against red, and all against each other.

My name is Fear, and I use the rich to despise the poor, the poor to despise the rich, and both to despise their reason!

My name is Fear, and I cut short long lives with presumption, not fact. My method is unique: I ease into sober minds and settle there and reason with existing hate, avarice and no knowledge.

I paint pictures of unseen things to make them real when, of course, they're not.

Then fools act on my suggestions and lay aside trust, which, only, is my enemy.

"For when it arrives, I must flee
or else be exposed by thee!"

HIS PASSING
(On the death of my father)

The news came like a fist slammed into an unsuspecting stomach. As quick as I could, I tried to compose my inner thoughts. All the unanswered questions raced through me, demanding acknowledgment, for which there were none!

He had died, this man called my "father." So many years had gone into emptiness, where past years go.

I tried to remember him. Something that would make me shed a tear. Force was no use; none came.

They told me it was "sudden," like all death not expected.

The final remains could be viewed if I hurried. What is it that remains, when all is final?

Still I wanted to see him, whose image neglect had worn away... or so I told myself. What I could do, I did: I drank!

My drunken image saw a child being held by him in a bar: him sitting on his throne, the child starting a career.

When at last I neared the place of his last remains, I turned and went another way.

His passing had occurred for me, so many years ago, when I needed an ear, a pat, a smile, a friend... a father.

I never knew where they laid him, how many carried him away. I only know that he has passed, and the drunken image will never do the same.

HOW SHE SLEW ME

It's not her smile that caused my death;
Her eyes, cunning ways, her sweet panting
breath.
No, not her lips, so full and so round,
Nor her keeping my heart on its merry go
round!

It wasn't the touch, with its softness unique;
Not the look in her eyes, that could lull me to
sleep.
No, not the finger that played with my hair
Or the things that she whispered that made
me to dare.

She slew me with something only love can
explain:
Slew me with kindness, exchanged for my
pain.
Removed my old heart, iron and cold;
Fashioned her love and gave me a soul.
And now, made over, someone brand new
Whose life now has purpose because he has
you.

Hooray for death; look what it's done.

In the touch of your kindness,
you've made me someone.

MY BROTHER
(On his passing)

He was my bigger half:

a kind of support, a staff,

the brother that made the word worthwhile

with a simple, illuminating smile!

The gift of music he did possess.

The Son of God, he did confess.

The piano was his claim to fame.

His music put learned men to shame.

Amazing how his fingers all would glide
across the keys on a downward slide.

The beauty from the melody played
made easy, for his fingers all obeyed!

He had gotten sick, sicker still; he knew:

Wasting away before our very view.

Yet, again God's grace on him bestowed,
and he came home, somewhat restored!

Back at music he loved so much;
back at the thing that obeyed his touch;

It was a winter's day, the kind you hate,
that he sat in a chair to await his fate.

I wonder where his thoughts were aimed
as he sat and waited with vision strained?

The call was soft, sure, and real:
a musician was needed with only his skill.

He plays, I believe, in the heavenly choir.
The music there, much more serene.

I see grinning, looking afar
at the one he loved, his Lord and King!

The choir is made up of ones once here.

From old Hickory and Singleton Street,
the piano won't fade, neither will he.

The songs he now plays, just continue their eternal beat.

MY NAME IS PRAYER

You need me when you are afraid that life has passed you by and the end was not prepared for.

You recite me when new jobs are needed and material things are scarce.

My name is Prayer.

I know you.

You call me in the night times, when you're alone in the dark and the boogie man is in your room.

My name is Prayer, and you use me at dinner tables, when others look at you and you attempt to show them how pious you can really be.

My name is Prayer, and I never come from make-believe aspirations with you as their goal. I come from anguished hurts, intense pain, mother's lost children, straying husbands, defeated dreams, death begging to win.

My name is Prayer.

I live to be used by fumbling words: lips that are formed but can't produce the sound, tears from places within not known before.

My name is Prayer, and only when the conditions are as they should be: broken spirit, pride abandoned, faith trusted in... only then do I speak with words the tongue has never learned!

VIETNAM, GIVE ME BACK MY FRIEND

We were young, naïve, unknowing, full of the dreams of life and what our paths would become.

My friend, whose name was Charles, was wide eyed, with the claims of life; looking forward to a world devoted to our aims, our ready desires.

We sipped red bottles of Wild Irish Rose wine, smoked our heavy-laced pungent sticks of weed, wrapped tightly in tightly-rolled Zig Zag papers. And under this stimulus, charged through life and dreams, as conquerors of our own fortunes, Viet Nam came.

How horrible the name! The sun now shone on our haggard brows; on, in fact, used up boys who had went away to get away...along with thousands more, of young dreamers, still asleep.

I missed him: my friend, my fellow traveler in our minds' depressions.

One night, I stood under my building's archway. It was cold. The air was stunning in its touch. And as I turned to complain to heaven, I saw him. His eyes were dark, devoid of fire, lacking life. He was thin, wispy, otherworldly in his gaze. He looked at me, through me, past me. He shook, not from the cold, but from a frightening need. He spoke of jungles, thick leaves, unbearable rain, cries of pain, shouts of death, fields of poppies, veins filled with dope.

I didn't know my friend. He left me again, smoking weed, sipping wine, dreaming. He had left me; he had left his spirit: it had died in Viet Nam.

LITTLE BLACK BOY

He arrived in my life when he was two
months old: small, and thin, both weak and
faint.

How did he manage to live from a crack
mom's fold –
neither rich
nor poor,
sinner or saint?

Why did I take him, this little black boy,
whose narrow-pointed head did hang;
whose body resembled a broken toy.
at whose birth, no joy bells rang?

But time has a way of breaking through,
creating in life a mystery.

For he laughed and smiled and ate and grew.

His antics and squeals became therapy.

He cried a lot; of course he did;
wet his pamper thru and thru.

sucked Enfamil like it had no lid and would
rub his hand in his "number 2!"

But at night in my bed and only with him
when all others had gone to sleep,
he would lay on my chest, watch the sun
slowly dim.

My heart would say softly, "Him you must
keep!"

I would take his big toe, snuggle it soft.

Then I'd tub my chin in his tummy for fun.

My prayer could be heard, as it hurtled aloft
knowing, for us, our day was done.

Little black boy, oh, little black boy,
how you changed my concept of life.

My son, my son, my little black joy,
what peace you've exchanged for my strife.

What is it like to not have a son?

You're an empty space, a barren land.

What is complete until the job is done
when a little black boy can define being a
man!

MY NAME IS GUN

Who me?
No one in particular:
separator of families,
creator of pain,
dissolver of dreams,
fixer of revenge,
exactor of retribution.

My name is Gun.

I find favor wherever I go.

My name is Gun.

I am old, tired, yet young and angry!

My name is Gun.

I sleep under pillows,
crawl into waist bands,
ride under shoulders,
hug your thighs,
drape your back,
lie next to your makeup.

My name is Gun.

I have few friends.

For some, I am as Brutus and Judas.

My name is Gun.

I am pretty. My neck can be long, warm, yet cold. My belly is round, a receptacle for whatever you wish to thrust in me. I will take any size!

My name is Gun.

I have no allegiance.

My back is firm. Squeeze me and I will respond. Some accuse me of pride, of ego, of having no shame.

My name is Gun.

I am never to blame. I speak, and disputes are settled, right or wrong. I separate families, lovers, friends.

If you treat me with contempt, I reply. Children love my luster, my quietness. The mistake of assuming my loneliness for friendship results in pain!

My name is Gun.

I quell. I sort. I end.

My history is longer than yours; my family line, more honored.

Diverse, we are.

Dangerous and deadly is our motto.

My name is Gun; my measurements cause envy in all women! .45, .38, .22, .35. My initials define me: 9mm; Mac 10; AK; S&W!

My name is Gun.

If you wish, I can be silenced.

Hold me.
Hide me.
Melt me.

Destroy me.

Make me over into cups that hold wine, braces for crooked legs.

I've caused chairs for backs.

I've made immobile, covers for lives.

I've ended, plagues for the innocent I've claimed.

My name is Gun!

REASON FOR PAIN

The reason for pain is to cause me to grow,
to discover my strength, my faults, my core.

The deeper the pain, the greater the need
To examine my reasons, vanity... greed.

Pain, at its best, stirs the pure soul;
makes either wiser or withers the whole.

Deep inside, hiding within hearts,
it tears at the strings, 'til the whole body
smarts.

The tears ensure, run like pure rain;
but that's the side issue, related to pain.
Mastered by it; destroyed by it too,
the results of its testing is that you're
made brand new!

HER PASSING

Something about that day was strange. It was not the chill, nor the silence of the familiar sounds that all Sunday mornings are known for. The Church was the same, as people slowly, even though late, came in quietly. They were ready to hear about the goodness of God and the blessings that awaited them in heaven. I was prepared to tell them!

It was as if time stopped and the waiting faces were frozen in anticipation. My mouth was open when someone said in a whispered tone into my ear, yet in my brain so loud, "Your mother has passed!"

Gasping for words, strangled on silence, I said to the waiting citizens of another world, "I must leave; mother has passed!"

Stunned, their heads dropped in disbelief that she would leave them here and go before them to the other side. My car excelled in speed and took me where she lay. I allowed it to do so, for I had no power to resist! In the crowded hall of death called a hospital, voices known and unknown competed for my ears. Fallen in my arms, baby sister could only look at me, not with eyes, but with wet, glazed orbs of sorrow.

I went into the small area behind a curtain that had been tattooed by so many hands that had pulled it back. She was still... quiet... sleep. My gaze could not awaken her; my promises to be good, neither could my prayers. How dark she had become, how old, how tired. It was the kiss I gave her, I shall never forget: a kiss she didn't acknowledge as she had before.

Surprisingly, I could only say, "I miss you," and turned and left, my sanity not to be found for many years.

The Journey

There is a journey we all must take,
filled with sights of skies and lakes.

Colors too, our views behold,
the wonders, never really told.

The journey starts with halting steps,
falling, crawling, with minor help.

Standing on our shaky legs,
A challenge in us starts to beg.

And so we walk, slow and sure,
meeting all, of life's allure.

Starry skies, cloudy days,
Rainy mornings, fogs with haze,
the journey takes us, miles around
old battered hearts, angry frowns.

Smiles of friends, cries of kin,
always facing life's chilling winds.

And so it ends, as journeys must,
with each returning to the dust.

We were once here; we saw it all.

Now we await, the Autumn's call.

Edward Blair

www.ingramcontent.com/pod-product-compliance
Lightning Source LLC
Chambersburg PA
CBHW061723020426
42331CB00006B/1062